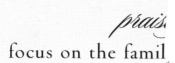 

This marriage study series is pure Focus on the Family—
reliable, biblically sound and dedicated to reestablishing
family values in today's society. This series will no doubt help a
multitude of couples strengthen their relationship, not only with
each other, but also with God, the *creator* of marriage itself.

Bruce Wilkinson

Author, The BreakThrough Series: *The Prayer of Jabez,
Secrets of the Vine* and *A Life God Rewards*

In this era of such need, Dr. Dobson's team has produced solid,
helpful materials about Christian marriage. Even if they have been
through marriage studies before, every couple—married or engaged—
will benefit from this foundational study of life together. Thanks to
Focus on the Family for helping set us straight in this top priority.

Charles W. Colson

Chairman, Prison Fellowship Ministries

In my 31 years as a pastor, I've officiated at hundreds of weddings.
Unfortunately, many of those unions failed. I only wish the *Focus on
the Family Marriage Series* had been available to me during those years.
What a marvelous tool you as pastors and Christian leaders have
at your disposal. I encourage you to use it to assist those you
serve in building successful, healthy marriages.

H. B. London, Jr.

Vice President, Ministry Outreach/Pastoral Ministries
Focus on the Family

Looking for a prescription for a better marriage?
You'll enjoy this timely and practical series!

Dr. Kevin Leman

Author, *Sheet Music: Uncovering the Secrets of
Sexual Intimacy in Marriage*

The *Focus on the Family Marriage Series* is successful because it shifts
the focus from how to fix or strengthen a marriage to *who* can do it.
Through this study you will learn that a blessed marriage will be the
happy by-product of a closer relationship with the *creator* of marriage.

Lisa Whelchel

Author, *Creative Correction* and
The Facts of Life and Other Lessons My Father Taught Me

In a day and age where the covenant of marriage is so quickly tossed
aside in the name of incompatibility and irreconcilable differences,
a marriage Bible Study that is both inspirational and practical
is desperately needed. The *Focus on the Family Marriage Series* is what
couples are seeking. I give my highest recommendation to this Bible
study series that has the potential to dramatically impact and improve
marriages today. Marriage is not so much about finding the right
partner but rather being the right partner. These studies give wonderful
biblical teachings for helping those who want to learn the beautiful art
of being and becoming all that God intends in their marriage.

Lysa TerKeurst

President, Proverbs 31 Ministries
Author, eight books including *Capture His Heart* and *Capture Her Heart*

the communicating *marriage*

Gospel Light

Gospel Light is a Christian publisher dedicated to serving the local church. We believe God's vision for Gospel Light is to provide church leaders with biblical, user-friendly materials that will help them evangelize, disciple and minister to children, youth and families.

It is our prayer that this Gospel Light resource will help you discover biblical truth for your own life and help you minister to others. May God richly bless you.

For a free catalog of resources from Gospel Light, please call your Christian supplier or contact us at 1-800-4-GOSPEL *or* www.gospellight.com.

PUBLISHING STAFF
William T. Greig, Chairman · **Dr. Elmer L. Towns,** Senior Consulting Publisher · **Bayard Taylor, M.Div.,** Senior Editor, Biblical and Theological Issues · **Virginia Starkey** and **Tom Stephen,** Contributing Writers

Library of Congress Cataloging-in-Publication Data
The communicating marriage.
　　p. cm. — (Focus on the Family marriage series)
　Includes bibliographical references.
　ISBN 0-8307-3359-0 (trade paper)
　1. Marriage—Biblical teaching. 2. Interpersonal communication—Biblical teaching. 3. Marriage—Religious aspects—Christianity. 4. Interpersonal communication—Religious aspects—Christianity. 5. Communication in marriage. I. Focus on the Family (Organization) II. Series.
　BS680.M35C66 2005
´248.8'44—dc22

　　　　　　　　　　　　　　　　　　　　　　　　　　　　2005026229

table of contents

foreword

The most urgent mission field on Earth is not across the sea or even across the street—it's right where you live: in your home and family. Jesus' last instruction was to "make disciples of all nations" (Matthew 28:19). At the thought of this command, our eyes look across the world for our work field. That's not bad; it's just not *all*. God intended the home to be the first place of Christian discipleship and growth (see Deuteronomy 6:4-8). Our family members must be the *first* ones we reach out to in word and example with the gospel of the Lord Jesus Christ, and the fundamental way in which this occurs is through the marriage relationship.

Divorce, blended families, the breakdown of communication and the complexities of daily life are taking a devastating toll on the God-ordained institutions of marriage and family. We do not need to look hard or search far for evidence that even Christian marriages and families are also in a desperate state. In response to the need to build strong Christ-centered marriages and families, this series was developed.

Focus on the Family is well known and respected worldwide for its steadfast dedication to preserving the sanctity of marriage and family life. I can think of no better partnership than the one formed by Focus on the Family and Gospel Light to produce the *Focus on the Family Marriage Series*. This series is well written, biblically sound and right on target for guiding couples to explore the foundation God has laid for marriage and to see Him as the role model for the perfect spouse. Through these studies, seeds will be planted that will germinate in your heart and mind for many years to come.

In our practical, bottom-line culture, we often want to jump over the *why* and get straight to the *what*. We think that by *doing* the six steps or *learning* the five ways, we will reach the goal. But deep-rooted growth is slower and more purposeful and begins with a well-grounded understanding of God's divine design. Knowing why marriage exists is crucial to making the how-tos more effective. Marriage is a gift from God, a unique and distinct covenant relationship through which His glory and goodness can resonate, and it is only through knowing the architect and His plan that we will build our marriage on the surest foundation.

God created marriage; He has a specific purpose for it, and He is committed to filling with fresh life and renewed strength each union yielded to Him. God wants to gather the hearts of every couple together, unite them in love and walk them to the finish line—all in His great grace and goodness.

May God, in His grace, lead you into His truth, strengthening your lives and your marriage.

Gary T. Smalley
Founder and Chairman of the Board
Smalley Relationship Center

introduction

At the beginning of creation God "made them male and female." "For this reason a man will leave his father and mother and be united to his wife, and the two will become one flesh." So they are no longer two, but one.

Mark 10:6-8

The Communicating Marriage can be used in a variety of situations, including small-group Bible studies, Sunday School classes or counseling or mentoring situations. An individual couple can also use this book as an at-home marriage-building study.

Each of the four sessions contains four main components.

Session Overview

Tilling the Ground
This is an introduction to the topic being discussed—commentary and questions to direct your thoughts toward the main idea of the session.

Planting the Seed
This is the Bible study portion in which you will read Scripture and answer questions to help discover lasting truths from God's Word.

Watering the Hope
This is a time for discussion and prayer. Whether you are using the study at home as a couple, in a small group or in a classroom setting, talking about the lesson with your spouse is a great way to solidify the truth and plant it deeply in your hearts.

Harvesting the Fruit
As a point of action, this portion of the session offers suggestions on putting the truth of the Word into action in your marriage relationship.

Suggestions for Individual Couple Study

There are at least three options for using this study as a couple.

- It may be used as a devotional study that each spouse would study individually through the week; then on a specified day, come together and discuss what you have learned and how to apply it to your marriage.
- You might choose to study one session together in an evening and then work on the application activities during the rest of the week.
- Because of the short length of this study, it is a great resource for a weekend retreat. Take a trip away for the weekend, and study each session together, interspersed with your favorite leisure activities.

Suggestions for Group Study

There are many ways that this study can be used in a group situation. The most common is in a small-group Bible study format, but it can also be used in an adult Sunday School class. However you choose to use it, there are some general guidelines to follow for group study.

- Keep the group small—five to six couples is probably the maximum.
- Ask couples to commit to regular attendance for the four weeks of the study. Regular attendance is a key to building relationships and trust in a group.
- Encourage participants *not* to share anything of a personal or potentially embarrassing nature without first asking the spouse's permission.
- Whatever is discussed in the group meetings is to be held in strictest confidence among group members only.

Suggestions for Mentoring or Counseling Relationships

This study also lends itself for use in relationships where one couple mentors or counsels another couple.

- A mentoring relationship, where a couple that has been married for several years is assigned to meet on a regular basis with a younger couple, could be arranged through a system set up by a church or ministry.
- A less formal way to start a mentoring relationship is for a younger couple to take the initiative and approach a couple that exemplifies a mature, godly marriage and ask them to meet with them on a regular basis. Or the reverse might be a mature couple that approaches a younger couple to begin a mentoring relationship.
- When asked to mentor, some might shy away and think that they could never do that, knowing that their own marriage is less than perfect. But just as we are to disciple new believers, we must learn to disciple married couples to strengthen marriages in this difficult world. The Lord has promised to be "with you always" (Matthew 28:20).
- Before you begin to mentor a couple, first complete the study yourselves. This will serve to strengthen your own marriage and prepare you for leading another couple.
- Be prepared to learn as much or more than the couple(s) you will mentor.

There are additional helps for mentoring relationships in *The Focus on the Family Marriage Ministry Guide*.

The *Focus on the Family Marriage Series* is based on Al Janssen's *The Marriage Masterpiece* (Wheaton, IL: Tyndale House Publishers, 2001), an insightful look at what marriage can—and should—be. In this study, we are pleased to lead you through the wonderful journey of discovering the joy in your marriage that God wants you to experience!

express love
openly

Like an apple tree among the trees of the forest is my lover among the young men.
I delight to sit in his shade, and his fruit is sweet to my taste.
He has taken me to the banquet hall, and his banner over me is love.
Song of Songs 2:3-4

Does the following sound familiar?

> We stood in the snow for hours, just talking. After dinner, I meant
> to say good night quickly, but instead we had a two-hour conversa-
> tion in front of her dorm. We talked about our families, our jobs,
> and about how we needed to get out of the snow, but neither of us
> wanted the date to end. When we kissed good night, I couldn't wait
> to get to my room so that I could call her and tell her what a won-
> derful time I had.

How about this?

> By the time I get home, all I want to do is sit in front of the televi-
> sion or the computer and relax. After spending my whole day with
> people, I don't have energy to listen or talk. I know I should talk
> with my wife, but I figure we can catch up this weekend.

Marriages begin with a man and a woman who are enthralled with one
another. When a man and a woman are dating, they long to be with their

beloved and just talk to one another. They love to simply say (and hear), "I love spending time with you."

Yet many marriages die a slow death because of a lack of communication. Couples may still talk about projects or kids or jobs, but they often stop communicating their love and desire for each other.

As Christians, we believe that it is important to spend time with God every day. Most of us realize that if we skip our daily time with the Lord or give Him a quick five minutes, our spiritual lives will be adversely affected. The same is true of marriage. Couples need to find time each day to communicate.

Although a lack of communication may kill a marriage, regular and consistent communication will bring it to life. Love must not be assumed or taken for granted. Love must be spoken.

Do you want to rediscover the amazing person you married? Do you want a marriage that not only survives but also thrives? To accomplish this goal, you and your spouse must do what you did when your relationship started: talk to each other.

 tilling the ground

Men and women have different needs for communicating. Stereotypes do not describe every individual person, but they do give a general picture of what's true about many of us. Most men prefer to communicate their love through actions, whereas many women enjoy communicating through words.

The bottom line is that we all need actions and words to grow in relationship with our spouse. We need each other to "talk the talk" and "walk the walk" in expressing our love to one another. That's what brought us together when we were dating, and that's what's going to deepen our marriage.

Let's explore the different ways we like to express and receive love.

1. List some ways that a dating couple demonstrates love for one another through their actions.

2. How do most dating couples use words to express their love for one another?

3. Do most married couples take their love for granted or do they actively seek to communicate their love for one another?

Why do you think that is?

4. If you could design the "perfect" marriage, how would the wife express her love to her husband?

How would the husband express his love to his wife?

None of us will ever have the perfect marriage, but we can experience the marriage that God intended for us as we follow His design and express our love for our spouse.

If you wanted to learn how to play basketball and Michael Jordan invited you to his house to give you a few pointers, would you go? If you wanted to learn about computers and Bill Gates offered to give you 12 free lessons and all the necessary equipment, would you take him up on the offer? If you were throwing a party and Martha Stewart offered to come to your house and show you the perfect recipes and decorations to impress your friends and family, would you say yes?

Michael, Bill and Martha are experts in their respective fields. If you get the chance to learn from the experts, it would be foolish not to take advantage of it.

At this point, you may be asking, "So who's the expert on expressing love?" You would be hard-pressed to find someone more experienced in expressing love than Jesus.

Jesus Is the Expert on Love

Do you remember the following scenario from the book of John? Jesus was having the worst night of his life. The religious leaders intended to put him to death. One of His good friends, Peter, watched closely as Jesus faced His accusers. Yet when asked if he knew Jesus, Peter denied his relationship with Jesus three times. As a result, Peter experienced intense isolation from his Lord and from God.

Fast-forward about a week and a half later and you find Jesus, Peter and some of the other disciples eating breakfast on the beach. Jesus had risen from the dead, as He had promised, and had come back to give some final words of instruction to His disciples.

5. Read John 21:15-19. Write down the ways Jesus encouraged Peter to express his love.

Why was it important for Peter to say three times that he loved Jesus?

Why do you think Jesus called Peter to do something in addition to saying that he loved Jesus?

6. Describe an experience in which you felt isolated in your marriage and either you or your spouse took a step to express love and perform a loving act. How did that move you from feeling isolated to feeling close again?

Jesus ended His seminar on love by telling Peter that his death would be an expression of love. Jesus gave His life as a demonstration of God's love for us. Peter, in turn, would give his life as an expression of his love for Jesus.

7. Write down some practical ways that a husband and a wife can die to themselves as an expression of love for one another.

Actions Speak Louder Than Words

The book of 1 Corinthians was a letter written by Paul to a church struggling to understand the gifts that God gives to people. In this letter, God gives us a wonderful definition of the word "love."

In this letter, Paul describes a type of love that the Greeks called *agape*, which we might call God's unconditional love. Paul explained that the most excellent gift that God has given to us is the opportunity to learn to love as He loves.

8. A "list poem" is a list of words or phrases that completes a given sentence. Use the definition of "love" found in 1 Corinthians 13:4-8 to help you write a list poem by completing the following two sentences:

I show love for someone when I . . .

I show love for someone when I do not . . .

Note: If you want to be creative, you can even create some images or use different colors to express what you are learning.

9. Take a moment to review the poems that you have written from Paul's definition of "agape."

What actions have you taken this past week that have demonstrated agape love to your spouse?

What would you like to do differently in the upcoming week?

Without Words, Actions Lose Their Meaning

Take a moment to read the verse at the beginning of this session. Are you surprised that the Bible has such a vivid expression of human love? Well, this is tame compared with some of the other images presented in this love poem called the Song of Songs.

One Bible scholar described the Song of Songs this way: "The Song celebrates the joy of physical touch, the exhilaration of exotic scents, the sweet sound of an intimate voice, the taste of another's body. Furthermore, the book explores human emotion—the thrill and power of love."[1]

God has given us the gift of romantic love. Openly expressing love through words will touch the part of your spouse's soul that longs to hear that he or she is loved and appreciated.

10. Read Song of Songs 5:10-16 (a woman's expression of love to her husband) and 6:4-9 (a man's expression of love to his beloved). What ways have you learned to express romance to your spouse with your words?

11. What happens to marriages that do not continue to develop a language of romance and appreciation?

Although the writer of Song of Songs seemed to love poetry and imagery, many of us are not as comfortable or as creative in expressing our love for our spouse in this way. But we can all learn to express love openly and often. One simple way is to practice saying, "I love you" and "I appreciate you" throughout the week.

12. During a given week, how often to you express love and appreciation to your spouse?

If you are uncomfortable expressing emotions such as love and appreciation to others, you are not alone. Many of us never learned to express these types of feelings when we were growing up, and that has influenced the way we communicate with our spouse. If you grew up in a family that experienced divorce or in which words of love were few and far between, expressing love may feel foreign to you.

Read the following case study and explore your feelings and thoughts about expressing love through words and actions.

Dave never questioned whether his parents loved him. He enjoyed a typical childhood of sports, family vacations, dinners at six every night and extended family gatherings during the holidays. His parents would occasionally have a disagreement, but they never fought. They also rarely showed outward signs of affection. It was an unspoken assumption that families love one another, and to say "I love you" would have been a little embarrassing.

The only emotions that were expressed openly were words of disapproval for how others dressed or acted that were different from how his family dressed and acted. Fortunately for Dave, however, his actions seemed to always please his parents—especially his mom.

When Lauren first met Dave, she felt a great sense of stability and security. During her childhood she had felt like a ship caught in a storm, never sure if she would ever find solid ground. Dave and his family gave her a port in which to rest. His family seemed so pleasant and caring. Dave also enjoyed making "cute" jokes that made Lauren laugh. Dave was everything Lauren had longed for as a child: stable, fun, serious. The fact that he was headed into the world of high finance only added to the attraction. Lauren had learned the art of adapting to her environment to fit in, and she quickly learned the "rules" of Dave's family that made him and his parents quite happy.

Soon after their honeymoon, Lauren began to sense something change in Dave's attitude toward her. As he worked his way up the financial ladder, he seemed to show less and less affection for her. She was surprised at how uncomfortable he became hugging her or even holding hands while they were at his parents' house. When she tried to express her feelings, his once "cute" little jokes became an annoying technique to avoid dealing with the problem.

Two years into the marriage, Lauren felt as though the emotion and love were completely absent. Dave became frustrated with her lack of interest in sex. Lauren made attempts to talk about her feelings, but Dave simply ignored them. After all, if she had a problem, she should try to solve it.

Lauren soon found herself seeking love and appreciation in a coworker. When she finally gave Dave the divorce papers, he was in total shock. He had thought everything was fine.

13. How did Dave's experience as a child affect the way he related to Lauren?

How did Lauren's experience as a child have an impact on the way she related to Dave?

14. If you were having coffee with Dave and he asked you for advice on how to best show love for Lauren, what would you tell him?

15. Remembering the conversation that Jesus had with Peter, what do you think Jesus would say to Dave?

What would He say to Lauren?

 harvesting the fruit

God and Our Parents Model Love

Our parents modeled for us how to express love to a spouse. Take a moment to reflect on what you learned as a child about how a husband and a wife express love to one another.

16. Describe how your father expressed (or didn't express) love to your mother through his words and actions.

Describe how your mother expressed (or didn't express) love to your father through her words and actions.

Do you see any similarities in how you express love in your marriage?

Do you see any differences?

17. Reread God's definition of "love" given in 1 Corinthians 13:4-8, and then write down two ways that you would like to put those words into action this week.

For the husband:
This week I will practice agape love for my wife by _____
_____and _____.

For the wife:
This week I will practice agape love for my husband by _____
_____and _____.

Are you ready to invest yourself in expressing love openly? Practice in this case may not make you perfect, but it will help you enjoy the gift of romantic love. Below is a list of simple ways to express your love for your spouse. As you review this list, decide in which ways you would like to express your love to your spouse this coming week.

- Say "I love you" every night before you fall asleep.
- Give your spouse an unexpected hug.
- Send your spouse an e-mail describing what you appreciate about him or her.
- Write your spouse a note expressing what you love about him or

her and let your spouse find it during the day.

- Say "thank you" at least five times each day for things you appreciate about your spouse.
- Create your own ways to express love.

A Date Encourages Communication

A great way to enrich your marriage is to spend time daily in God's Word. Below is a list of Scriptures that you may choose to meditate on each day as a reminder of God's love for you and of your love for your spouse. As you meditate on these passages during the week, watch for how God will use this time to help you better express your love to your spouse.

> Day 1: Psalm 18:1
> Day 2: Psalm 116:1
> Day 3: Isaiah 43:4
> Day 4: Isaiah 54:10
> Day 5: Jeremiah 31:3
> Day 6: Psalm 31:21
> Day 7: Psalm 89:1

Another great way to rediscover the joy of communication is to ask your spouse out on a date. A date is a wonderful way to be intentional about taking the time to talk. This date could involve simply going on a short walk in the evening or sharing a cup of coffee in the morning. Be sure to begin your date with prayer. Prayer not only will deepen your relationship with God, but it will also deepen your relationship with one another.

This week, we will have a date on _____, and we will

_____.

Note

1. Tremper Longman III, *Song of Songs* (Grand Rapids, MI: William B. Eerdmans Publishing Company, 2001), p. 59.

deal with problems *honestly*

Let the word of Christ dwell in you richly as you teach and admonish one another with all wisdom, and as you sing psalms, hymns and spiritual songs with gratitude in your hearts to God.
Colossians 3:16

On May 11, 1981, the world mourned the death of international reggae star Bob Marley. From a humble beginning in Jamaica, Bob Marley and the Wailers had brought the sound of reggae to the airwaves with hits such as "I Shot the Sheriff." Marley's death was attributed to cancer in his liver and brain.

Doctors had first discovered the cancer in 1977—at that time, it was isolated in Marley's big toe. However, instead of seeking medical attention when the cancer was still treatable, Marley ignored the advice of doctors and continued to tour and perform. When the cancer became too much for Marley to bear, he finally had to face the reality of his disease. By then it was too late—the cancer had spread to the rest of his body. Bob Marley died at the age of 36 because of a disease that began in his big toe.[1]

When couples do not honestly talk about problems and difficult life issues, those problems (which may be very treatable in the early stages) can become a cancer that consumes the relationship. Often couples forgo openly communicating about problems, believing that the problems will solve themselves. A lack of honest communication will prevent you and your spouse from enjoying the healthy relationship that God intended for you both.

Do you know what a blue whale, a mountain goat and a fox have in common? They all respond to problems with the same two instincts: *fight* or *flight*. God designed animals to protect themselves by either beating down their opponent or by running away. We've been given a similar instinct, but we've also been given the gift of communication. We can face problems without the need to fight or flee.

1. Make a list of problems or difficult life situations that most married couples face during their marriage.

2. What are some ways that married couples avoid authentic communication about these problems by relying on the *fight* instinct?

3. What are some ways married couples avoid communication by relying on the *flight* instinct?

4. Where would you place yourself on the fight-flight continuum in the way that you and your spouse normally face problems or difficult situations?

Fight	Honest Communication	Flight
Discuss in order to get your way	Discuss in order to come together	Avoid discussion of problems

When Adam and Eve ate the forbidden fruit, humanity experienced separation from God and also inherited the reality that we will all face problems (see Genesis 3:14-16). But just as God provided for Adam and Eve and made a way for us all to be drawn back to Him through Christ, He has also given us extremely practical advice about how we can deepen our relationship with our spouse as we authentically face our problems together.

planting the seed

In the book of Revelation, Jesus sends a "State of the Union" letter to the church at Ephesus. Can you imagine what Jesus would say if He were to write a "State of Your Marriage" letter to you? Would you open it right away, or would you tuck it under a pile of letters and open it at a later date?

The church in Ephesus knew how to confront problems honestly. In fact, the members of the church in Ephesus were experts. Their commitment to God and desire for purity guided them through many difficult situations. However, the church had one major problem.

5. Read Revelation 2:1-5 and then discuss how the Ephesians were not living as God intended. When you address problems without placing God first, what usually happens?

6. In verse 5, what two commands does Jesus give to the church?

How would returning to a love relationship with God have an impact on your ability to honestly confront problems?

In Revelation 2 and 3, Jesus demonstrates a wonderful pattern for deepening our relationship with God and with each other. This pattern is as follows:

First: Identify what is good in the relationship.
Second: Honestly identify problems in the relationship.
Third: Work toward solutions to help the situation.

Everyone experiences problems. Just as we need to be honest with God when we feel distant or frustrated, we need to practice the same pattern of communication with our spouse. We need to talk about problems such as a difficult medical diagnosis, the potential loss of a job, or a misunderstanding that has come up in the relationship.

Explore Paul's Instructions

In his letter to the Ephesians, Paul gives a dynamic description of a church in which the Jews and Gentiles did not get along (a common cause of problems in the first-century church). To confront the problem, Paul describes the Ephesians' relationship with God and how God made each of them one. Paul then offers some practical advice to help them live together in unity.

We will begin to explore Paul's instructions from Ephesians 4:25—5:2 in this session and then complete our study of this passage in session 3. To prepare for this study (and the next session's study), read the entire passage of Scripture (out loud would be ideal) and briefly talk with your spouse about what words or phrases stand out in your mind.

Let's take a look at the first two commands. Note that Paul begins with a negative command and then moves to a positive command. In other words, he first describes the problem and then offers a solution.

Therefore each of you must put off falsehood and speak truthfully to his neighbor, for we are all members of one body (4:25).

7. What are some of the ways in which you have not spoken honestly about the problems in your marriage?

What was the result?

8. How would the reminder that we are "one" in marriage help you to speak the truth to your spouse?

In your anger do not sin. Do not let the sun go down while you are still angry, and do not give the devil a foothold (4:26-27).

9. How have you used anger when discussing problems in your marriage?

How has anger prevented an honest discussion of problems in your marriage?

Simply put, we cannot do all that God commands us to do on our own. We need to ask the Holy Spirit to fill us with love, forgiveness and honesty. Remember, the problems in Ephesus began when the Ephesians forgot their first love: the love they received from God. If we want to communicate effectively with our spouse, we must return to that first love.

10. Read Ephesians 2:8-10. In what ways have you experienced God's grace through your marriage?

In verse 10, we read that God made us for good works. Those good works include effectively confronting problems.

11. How would having a closer relationship with God help you to speak honestly with your spouse and not sin in your anger?

12. Take a moment to pray for your spouse so that he or she might understand the fullness of God's love that comes through Jesus Christ.

 watering the hope

God has given us many tools to use as we communicate with our spouse. One very effective tool that we can use to help others understand our feelings is through emotional word pictures. In their book *The Language of Love: How to Quickly Communicate Your Feelings and Needs*, Gary Smalley and John Trent write, "emotional word pictures can enrich your every conversation and relationship. That is, they will enable your words to penetrate the heart of your listener—to the extent that your listener will truly understand and even feel the impact of what you say."[2]

In the following story, consider how Tricia effectively communicates with her husband, Dale, as they face a growing problem in their marriage:

Once again, Tricia felt that her husband, Dale, was slipping away. Years before, their marriage had almost ended because Dale was spending most of his time and emotional energy at work. When Tricia let Dale know that she intended to take their daughter and leave the marriage, Dale "woke up" and sought help. A professional counselor helped him establish new patterns of work. A spiritual director helped him confront his sin and brokenness before God. Not only did Tricia stay, but she and Dale also discovered the loving marriage that they felt God had intended for them from the beginning.

However, when Dale took on a new position at work, things began to slip. He soon fell back into old patterns, and Tricia began to once again experience her old feelings of resentment. Attempts at facing the problem fell on deaf ears as Dale walked blindly back into being consumed by work. Tricia's anger and frustration just seemed to increase the distance between them.

To communicate her feelings to Dale, Tricia decided to use the following word picture:

Dale, imagine that I had an affair a couple of years ago, and you decided to do the hard work of forgiving me and working on our marriage. I changed my ways and not only broke off the relationship with the other man, but also placed my energy and love into you. In fact, I stopped meeting with any man without your knowledge, and we talked openly about what I did during the day. You began to trust that I was totally committed to you.

Now imagine that you are downtown one day and see me in a restaurant with another man. Maybe he's a friend of the family—someone you know has a tendency to flirt with women. You walk up to the table and you notice that our hands are touching. How would you feel? What if I told you that nothing was happening and that your feelings were wrong because, after all, I had changed? What if that happened three times in two weeks? Every time you talked to me about it, I told you that the problem was with you because, after all, I had changed. What would you think? How would you feel? What if you walk-ed in the house one day and found me alone with the same man? We were simply talking on the couch. How would you feel?

That's how I'm feeling about your work right now. I want to trust that things are okay, but I feel like you are flirting with old patterns again.

After Dale heard this word picture, he began to listen. Tricia and Dale were able to have an honest talk about what was happening with his work.

13. How would you describe Tricia's attempts to talk with Dale about their problem?

Why do you think Dale was unable to "hear" her?

14. If you were Dale, how would you have received Tricia's word picture?

15. How does this case study demonstrate the ability to speak the truth and not let anger become sin?

As you consider what you've learned about confronting problems from Scripture and from Dale and Tricia's story, you may feel God leading you to openly discuss problems in your marriage. If so, get ready for some good but difficult times as you grow closer to one another.

harvesting the fruit

We've discovered that Jesus gave us a pattern for communication that can strengthen both our relationship with God and our relationship with our spouse. Take time to work through the following exercises as a first step in deepening those relationships.

First: Identify What Is Good in the Relationship

16. Imagine what God might write to you if He were describing what is good about your relationship with Him and with other people. Write that letter.

17. Write a short note to your spouse describing what is positive about your relationship.

Second: Honestly Identify Problems in the Relationship

18. Imagine what God might write to you if He were describing a problem in your relationship with Him. Write that note.

19. Write a short note to your spouse describing a problem or difficult situation that you are facing in your marriage.

Third: Work Toward Solutions to Help the Situation

20. Imagine what God might write if He were to give you a solution to a problem in your relationship with Him. Write that note.

21. Write a short note to your spouse describing what you can do to help bring a resolution to a problem in your relationship. Do not identify what your spouse needs to do, but simply identify what you need to do.

Together with your spouse, share the notes you wrote describing what is positive about your relationship. If you have time, you may want to create an emotional word picture that will help your spouse understand how you feel about him or her.

After sharing those notes, pray for God's guidance as you discuss the problems you have written down. This may be difficult, so don't rush. After praying, share the notes you wrote identifying a problem within your relationship. Repeat what your spouse says and ask a clarifying question or two to be sure that you understand your spouse's feelings about the problem.

Now share the ways you intend to work on the problem. After hearing what your spouse intends to do, begin the process of talking about what small steps you both might take to continue to talk and pray about this particular situation.

Experience God's Blessing

Remember the note Jesus wrote to the Ephesians? Well, He also gave them a word of encouragement:

> He who has an ear, let him hear what the Spirit says to the churches. To him who overcomes, I will give the right to eat from the tree of life, which is in the paradise of God (Revelation 2:7).

If you want to eat from the tree of life and experience the blessing that God has for your marriage, you must be willing to go the distance. The concept of overcoming involves being willing to work through problems and to stay committed to your relationships with both God and your spouse.

Are you willing to overcome problems in your marriage? You've made a good first step by identifying what is good, talking about a specific problem and working toward a solution. Now you need to make a commitment to working through the problem.

22. Describe ways that your spouse can help you stay committed to working through problems in your marriage.

23. Describe actions that you can take to help you and your spouse develop the ability to honestly talk about problems during the coming years.

A great way to stay committed to talking about problems is to set aside time each week to have a "couple check-in." During this time you can pray together, talk about what is going well in your relationship that week and discuss any problems that might be developing. When you establish a time to check in, be sure to also plan an activity that you both enjoy. One way to remember your first love in marriage is to have fun and laugh.

During the next month, we will take time to check in on _____.

After checking in, we will then spend time together by _____.

Notes

1. *Wikipedia,* "Bob Marley: Battle with Cancer." http://en.wikipedia.org/wiki/Bob_Marley#Battle_with_cancer (accessed August 2005).
2. Gary Smalley and John Trent, *The Language of Love: How to Quickly Communicate Your Feelings and Needs* (Colorado Springs, CO: Focus on the Family Publishers, 1999), n.p.

express emotions
appropriately

We wait in hope for the Lord; he is our help and our shield. In him our
hearts rejoice, for we trust in his holy name.
Psalm 33:20-21

My heart is in anguish within me; the terrors of death assail me. Fear and
trembling have beset me; horror has overwhelmed me.
Psalm 55:4-5

Imagine a world without color. Imagine a world with only shades of black and white. What do you think life would be like if it looked like a television rerun from the 1950s? Pretty boring, huh?

God created endless shades of color. Color not only adds variety to our lives, but color also speaks to our souls. Have you ever seen a rainbow after a huge storm? Or a forest of golden elm trees at the peak of fall? God gave the world the gift of color.

Now imagine a world without any emotions. Imagine a world in which tears, laughter, anger and joy did not exist. What do you think life would be like if we simply related to others as impersonal robots, without feelings? Pretty boring, huh?

God gave us many emotions and feelings. Emotions not only add variety to our lives, but they also allow our souls to speak. When we avoid our emotions, we reject a gift God gave us to deepen our relationship with others.

To experience healthy communication within marriage, we need to be able to express our emotions. We need to be free to share hurts, concerns and joys in a safe environment with our spouse. As we express and experience these gifts that God gave us, our marriage will experience the full life that Jesus promised (see John 10:10).

tilling the ground

> *The heart is forever inexperienced.*
> —Henry David Thoreau[1]

> *Emotions are alien to me. I'm a scientist.*
> —Spock, "This Side of Paradise," Stardate 3417.3, *Star Trek* [2]

These quotations represent two extremes in approaching emotions. Henry David Thoreau spent the last part of his life seeking to understand the fullness of emotion and feeling. In fact, his poetry gave a voice to an entire generation of young people longing to feel and experience life. Spock (a character from the original *Star Trek*), on the other hand, lived a life devoid of emotions. Spock represents the impersonal and purely logical approach to life.

1. In your childhood home, did you learn to be more like Thoreau (express all your feelings) or Spock (express no emotion, just logic)?

   What did that feel like?

2. Describe a situation in which expressing emotions damaged a relationship.

   Describe a situation in which expressing emotions strengthened a relationship.

3. Describe a situation in which withholding emotions damaged a relationship.

   Describe a situation in which tempering an emotion strengthened a relationship.

4. Make a list of the conditions that are helpful in creating a situation for a healthy expression of feelings.

When Adam first saw Eve, he trembled with joy. Humans were created to express themselves openly (see Genesis 2:23-25). A lot has changed since then.

As with all of God's creation, emotions have been affected by our separation from God. Although Adam may have expressed himself perfectly when he first met Eve, everything changed when he and Eve disobeyed God and sin entered the world. Suddenly, women and men felt a variety of new emotions (anger, guilt, shame), and those emotions were tainted by a sinful nature.

In this study, you will learn not only to enjoy the variety of emotions that God gave us, but also to express them in a way that honors God and helps you develop a stronger relationship with your spouse.

 planting the seed

> *It is my view, that in the words of this book, the whole of human life, its basic spiritual conduct and as well its occasional movements and thoughts is comprehended and contained. Nothing to be found in human life is omitted.*
> —Athanasius, *Ad Marcellinum*[3]

Can you imagine a book that contains everything we may experience as a human being?

The psalms in the Bible wonderfully model the variety of emotions known to humanity. The psalmists never pulled punches: When they were angry, they expressed it. When they were disheartened or depressed, they mourned. When they were filled with joy, they praised God.

5. Read each verse from Psalms below. Write down two or three words that describe the emotions each verse reflects.

    Psalm 1:1-2

    Psalm 12:1

    Psalm 23:1-3

    Psalm 40:17

Psalm 51:4-5

Psalm 84:1-2

Psalm 116:1-4

Psalm 126:2-3

Psalm 137

Psalm 150

Now that we've explored some of the emotional colors in Scripture, let's take a closer look at one psalm in particular: Psalm 55.

Wounds That Go Deep

As a young boy, David spent his days and nights watching the sheep. During his time alone in the fields, David developed an intimate love relationship with God. David knew God's protection and believed that God would always be with him. When David became a man, God established a covenant with David, promising to always be with him (see 2 Samuel 7:8-17).

How did David develop such a close relationship with God? He learned to express all his emotions. When David was afraid, he told God. When David was joyful, he told God. When David had a problem, he told God.

Psalm 55 illustrates how to develop intimacy in a relationship by openly expressing our emotions in a safe environment.

6. Take a moment to read Psalm 55 slowly out loud. Let the words rest in your spirit. Read the psalm a second time and write down the emotions that David expresses toward God.

7. How do David's emotions change as he progresses through the psalm?

8. From your experience, how does sharing your feelings with someone you love help to draw you closer to that person?

To be able to trust, David needed to be honest with God about his feelings of fear and abandonment. David had to walk through the valley of emotional darkness to find the light on the other side. The same is true in our relationship with our spouse. There will be times when we need to work through difficult feelings to experience a closer relationship on the other side.

Psalm 55 not only highlights David's relationship with God, but it also tells us about a friend who betrayed David (see vv. 12-15).

9. Describe David's feelings toward this close friend who betrayed him.

10. How does David's desire for this friend (turned enemy) compare with what Jesus said in Matthew 5:43-48 about how we should treat those who have hurt us?

Psalm 55:15 gives a vivid picture of David's hatred toward those who have hurt him. In marriage, we encounter circumstances in which we feel disappointed or frustrated with the one we love. From feelings of disappointment when our spouse is late (again) to deep feelings of betrayal because of adultery, all married couples will experience difficulty in their marriage. Fortunately, God gives us some practical advice to express our emotions.

In order to discover God's plan, let's turn back to our friends in the ancient city of Ephesus. We started our study of this passage in session 2. Once again, read Ephesians 4:25—5:2.

Now, let's take a closer look at this Scripture.

> *Do not let any unwholesome talk come out of your mouths, but only what is helpful for building others up according to their needs, that it may benefit those who listen* (4:29).

11. What's the difference between addressing a problem with the intention of strengthening your relationship with your spouse and wanting to simply express how you are feeling?

12. Is it possible to express feelings of frustration, fear and anger in a gracious way?

How have you experienced that graciousness?

And do not grieve the Holy Spirit of God, with whom you were sealed for the day of redemption (4:30).

Did you know that when you became a Christian, God's Spirit came alongside you to assist you in living a life that is pleasing to God? Jesus described the Holy Spirit as a *paraclete*, which literally means "one called to come alongside." The Holy Spirit will literally walk with you as you seek to love your spouse.

13. What actions would you associate with the expression "grieve the Holy Spirit"?

Get rid of all bitterness, rage and anger, brawling and slander, along with every form of malice (4:31).

14. What are some ways you have found helpful in putting away harmful reactions to your spouse so that you are able to communicate in a loving way?

Be kind and compassionate to one another, forgiving each other, just as in Christ God forgave you. Be imitators of God, therefore, as dearly loved children and live a life of love, just as Christ loved us and gave himself up for us as a fragrant offering and sacrifice to God (4:32—5:2).

Nothing can separate you from the love of God (see Romans 8:38-39). In Christ, we find forgiveness for the sins that we commit either by intention or by omission. God is committed to a lifelong relationship with you, and He knows that this relationship will include a lot of forgiveness. After all, nobody is perfect.

God's commitment to us models our commitment to our spouse. Just as God forgives us, we are to forgive our spouse.

15. How does the knowledge of God's forgiveness help you to be able to forgive your spouse?

16. If you cultivate an atmosphere of forgiveness in your marriage, how will that affect your ability to express all your emotions?

watering the hope

If we are passive and avoid our feelings, never expressing our feelings of love or frustration, our marriages will grow cold. If we express every emotion we have in an aggressive manner, the strength of our emotions could cause our spouse to turn away out of fear. A passive or an aggressive response to emotions will eventually cause isolation in our marriage.

If we acknowledge and assertively express with our spouse the feelings that God gave us, we will discover a deep level of intimacy. As you read the following case study, think about how Robert and Diane practice aggressive, passive and assertive approaches to their emotions.

Robert's Perspective

When Diane and Robert were first married, they enjoyed an active sex life. Even though Robert expected sex every day, they fell into a pattern of four times a week that felt good to him.

When Diane changed jobs and began to work longer hours, their sex life began to change. She was often too tired to have sex, which became a source of great frustration for Robert. When

Diane said no, Robert would make hurtful comments or simply get angry. After months of frustration, Robert simply gave up. He grew tired of being angry, so he simply began to watch television late into the night when Diane went to bed early. They both missed the closeness they once shared, but neither of them said anything.

Diane's Perspective

When Robert and Diane were first married, they spent what felt like hours talking about their day during breakfast and dinner. Together, they would plan house projects and vacations and talk about their work day. Their daily check-ins were the highlight of their married life.

When Diane changed jobs at Robert's request so that they could buy their first house, she felt the stress and time commitment of working in a more demanding work environment. When she arrived home, she secretly hoped that Robert would have dinner ready, but she was often disappointed to find him at the computer answering e-mail, with no meal prepared. She said nothing and went to work preparing the meal. When Diane tried to talk about her day, Robert's eyes would glaze over. She found herself getting more and more frustrated and tried to express this to him, but the conversation would quickly turn into a fight.

By the time Diane finished washing the dishes and getting herself ready for the next day, Robert was usually preoccupied with his favorite television show. Each night, she said, "Good night," hoping he would join her; but he only grunted.

17. If you were talking to Robert, what advice would you give him about expressing his emotions toward Diane in an assertive way?

What could Robert have done to create an environment in which Diane would understand his emotions?

18. If you were talking to Diane, what advice would you give her about expressing her emotions toward Robert in an assertive way?

What could Diane have done to create an environment in which Robert would understand her feelings?

19. Quickly review Ephesians 4:25—5:2. What advice would God give to Diane and Robert so that they might move toward intimacy?

20. On the scale below, how would you describe how you most often express your emotions toward your spouse?

Passive	Assertive	Aggressive
(Just deal with it)	(Open and caring)	(Loud, vocal, angry)

harvesting the fruit

Samuel Shoemaker once said, "Don't pray to escape trouble. Don't pray to be comfortable in your emotions. Pray to do the will of God in every situation. Nothing else is worth praying for."[4]

One way to create a safe place to talk with your spouse about your feelings is through prayer. God's will for you and your spouse is that you forgive each other and that you imitate God in how you speak and listen to one another. As you begin this section on identifying and expressing your emotions, take a moment to create an atmosphere in which you sense the presence of Christ through prayer.

Emotion Identification

Most of us have a hard time expressing our emotions because we have a hard time identifying our feelings. Generally, women have an easier time identifying and expressing their emotions, although this is changing. Below is a list of words that describe various emotions. After reading through them, use these words (and others that you may add) to identify how you are feeling about certain aspects of your relationship.

abandoned	afraid	alone	anxious
appreciative	ashamed	balanced	cheerful
confident	contemptuous	content	delighted
depressed	desolate	detached	disgraced
ecstatic	empty	excited	fearful
fortunate	glad	grand	grateful
hopeful	hopeless	insecure	judged
left out	magnificent	nervous	pleased
positive	remorseful	sad	safe
scared	sensational	sorrowful	tense
thankful	thrilled	timid	undeserving

21. Complete the following sentences to identify how you are feeling:

a. In general, two words that best describe how I feel about my marriage are_____ and _____.

b. When I think about our financial future, I often feel _____ and _____.

c. When I think about my relationship with God, I feel _____ and _____.

d. When I think about the future, I feel _____ and _____.

22. Choose one of the areas listed above and take time to explain to your spouse how and why you feel the way you are feeling. As you talk, remember that this is not a time to blame or fix a problem but simply a time to explain how you are feeling.

After you've each had a chance to explain your emotions, ask your spouse what actions you might take to bring intimacy into your relationship. After you've listened to your spouse, complete the following sentence:

In order to enhance our emotional relationship, my spouse would like me to _____ as a way of acknowledging his or her feelings about our marriage.

23. As a couple, reread Ephesians 4:25—5:2. What parts of this Scripture passage apply to your marriage and the issues you've been discussing?

Schedule a time during the coming week for you and your spouse to meet and follow up on what you've talked about today. It will be important to continue to meet together to talk openly about your marriage.

This week we will meet on _____ at _____ to talk about _____.
After our time of prayer and discussion, we will also _____, just for fun.

Notes

1. Henry David Thoreau, quoted at *Proverbia.net,* "Emotions." http://en.proverbia.net/citastema.asp?tematica=385&ntema=Emotions (accessed May 4, 2005).

2. *Quotable online.* http://www.quotableonline.com/Emotions.html (accessed May 4, 2005).

3. Athanasius, *Ad Marcellinum,* quoted in James L. Mays, *Psalms: Interpretation Commentary* (Louisville, KY: John Knox Press, 1994), p. 1.

4. Samuel Shoemaker, quoted at *Famous Quotes.* http://home.att.net/~quotations/religious.html (accessed May 5, 2005).

remember the past and *dream* for the *future*

*Remember the wonders [the Lord] has done, his miracles,
and the judgments he pronounced. Give thanks to the Lord,
for he is good; his love endures forever.*
1 Chronicles 16:12,34

A famous Chinese proverb reads, "If you want to know your past, look into your present conditions. If you want to know your future, look into your present actions."[1]

Have you found yourself wondering how you became the victim of a marriage that is slowly falling apart? Or maybe you've been overwhelmed by feelings of love and gratitude for a marriage that is thriving. If you take time to remember the past, you'll discover God's footprints in times of great joy and deep sorrow. You'll also discover that past decisions and actions have led you directly to where you are today.

Just as the past leads us to the present, the present will lead us into the future. Engaged couples often talk about their dreams for marriage. As life gets busy with jobs, kids and the stress of maintaining a household, few couples take the time to dream and plan for how they would like their relationship to develop. And for some, the Old Testament proverb "Where there is no vision, the people perish" (Proverbs 29:18, *KJV*) becomes a reality. Marriages without dreams grow distant. Healthy communication in marriage includes dreaming dreams, praying for the future and making plans to live out the marriage that God intends.

God gave the people of Israel an amazing promise. They were separated from God because of decisions in the past, but in the midst of their exile, God told them, "For I know the plans I have for you . . . plans to prosper you and not to harm you, plans to give you hope and a future" (Jeremiah 29:11). God's plans for your marriage are similar. As you seek to understand your past and dream about your future, you will discover a marriage that is good and prosperous.

tilling the ground

A famous hymn put it this way:

> Are you ever burdened with a load of care?
> Does the cross seem heavy, you are called to bear?
> Count your blessings, every doubt will fly,
> And you will keep singing as the days go by.
>
> Count your blessings, count them one by one.
> Count your blessings, see what God has done.
> Count your blessings, count them one by one.
> Count your many blessings, see what God has done.[2]

A great way to start thinking about your past is to simply "count your blessings."

1. What blessings have you experienced as a result of being with your spouse?

2. After considering those blessings, complete the following sentences:

The first time I knew I wanted to date my spouse was

_____.

I realized that I wanted to marry my spouse when

_____.

The greatest blessing in my marriage so far has been

_____.

One of the hardest situations that we have faced in our marriage has
been _____.

3. Describe a defining moment from your past.

    Did you have a sense of God's presence in that moment? If so, how was
    God working? If not, has your view of God's work changed over time?

4. What unrealistic expectations do most engaged couples have for their
    marriage?

5. What dreams do most married couples hope for in their marriage?

The psalms were God's original worship praise songs. The psalms gave structure and form to Hebrew worship that for thousands of years literally guided people into praise and remembrance. A central theme in both Christian and Hebrew worship is the concept of remembering. From God's command to the people of Israel to remember the exodus (see Deuteronomy 6:12) to Jesus' establishing the Lord's supper (see Mark 14:22-25), remembering God's work has been a vital element in a person's ability to communicate effectively with God.

Psalm 136 tells the story of God's faithfulness to the people of Israel. This psalm expresses how the Israelites counted their many blessings.

A good way to encounter this Psalm is to read it aloud. If possible, one person can read the first verse and another can say the phrase "His love endures forever." Notice that God's faithfulness includes both good times and difficult times.

6. After reading Psalm 136 aloud, write down your thoughts and feelings about God's ability to work in the life of the Israelites.

7. Why would it be important for the Israelites to pray through this psalm regularly?

How does remembering the past give a person hope for the future?

Psalm 136 progresses from God's work in the universe (vv. 1-9) to God's work in the life of God's people (vv. 10-22) to God's work in the life of individuals (vv. 23-25).

8. How can the progression of God's works in the universe to God's work in the lives of individuals help you reflect on how God has worked in your marriage?

A New Adventure

> *[The Lord] gave their land as an inheritance, His love endures forever. [A]n inheritance to his servant Israel; His love endures forever* (Psalm 136:21-22).

The Israelites went from being slaves in Egypt to being heirs of a great land. After years in the desert, God led them to a new land—a new adventure. To prepare for this new adventure, the Israelites were called to remember the past in order to take action in the present and, in so doing, prepare for the future.

9. Read Deuteronomy 6:1-12. Describe the ways that God encouraged the people of Israel to remember their past, act in the present and move toward the future.

Deuteronomy 6:4 begins with God calling the people of Israel to "hear." Israel's first step in experiencing God's blessing on this new adventure was listening. In many ways, the gift of communication in our marriages also begins with listening—listening to God and then to one another.

For some people, listening to God first as a way to prepare for the future of their marriage feels like a new and exciting adventure. We can learn a lot by understanding how God instructed the Israelites in their adventure.

How did God call the people of Israel to remember the past in order to prepare for the future? By talking about God's faithfulness and thinking through it at different points in the day, the Israelites were preparing to live in a land filled with milk and honey.

10. How might imagining the future of our marriage as "a land flowing with milk and honey" (Exodus 3:8) help us to see our futures differently?

11. List any aspect of your marriage that might be hindering your ability to see the future of your marriage as a promised land.

God's offer to bless the people of Israel came as a gift. God offers the same gift to each of us. We will experience God's blessing on our marriage as we follow the design He has given us—the design that will keep our relationship with Him and with our spouse growing and thriving. So, how do we do that? Let's take a look at what God had to say to the churches in the book of Revelation.

Overcomers Anonymous

The book of Revelation was originally written during the first century to churches that were struggling to stay faithful in the adventure of following God. Today, the prophetic passages of this book continue to have a tremendous impact on how we view God's work in the world.

Chapters 2 and 3 of Revelation describe specific words given by Jesus to seven first-century churches. Each church faced a different problem, yet each was given very similar advice on how to effectively live out God's dream.

12. Read Revelation 2:7,17; 3:21-22. What are the two ways Jesus encouraged the churches to act so that they could live out God's plan for the future?

The word "overcome" means to repent.[3] For the churches to move toward God's promises of the future, they needed to repent of what they had been doing wrong. In marriage, often the best way to begin to experience God's blessing toward the future is to repent or to turn away from unhealthy patterns of behavior and communication.

13. As you think through what you've learned throughout this study, what areas of your marriage do you sense God is calling you to overcome?

Jesus also said to the churches, "He, who has an ear to hear, let him hear what the Spirit is saying" (Revelation 2:7; 3:22). As with the people of Israel, the first step in healthy communication is to listen to what God has to say.

14. In your marriage, do you sense that God might be calling you to some new adventure?

15. Take a moment to ask God's Spirit to speak specifically to you and to your spouse. Individually, write down what you sense God is calling you to in the future.

God often uses images, or word pictures, to describe His blessings. We've already experienced the concept of "a land flowing with milk and honey" (Exodus 3:8). In the passages from Revelation, we see God's blessing described in a variety of ways that would make sense to the specific churches. Revelation

2:7 reads, "To him who overcomes, I will give the right to eat from the tree of life, which is in the paradise of God." In Genesis 2:9, we see that the "tree of life" is a gift given to the first married couple. The tree is also mentioned in Revelation 22:2. In that passage, the leaves are said to bring healing. Repentance will bring healing to broken relationships, with God and with your spouse.

Revelation 2:17 reads, "To him who overcomes, I will give some of the hidden manna. I will also give him a white stone with a new name written on it." The image of hidden manna refers to when the people of Israel were wandering through the desert and God provided food, called manna (see Exodus 16:4). God provided healthy food. Repentance is the healthy food from heaven that God has given you to prepare for the future.

In the first century, it was a common practice to give someone of valor a white stone. And if someone recovered from a serious injury, they were given a new name.[4] The images of repentance bring both health and newness to marriages.

 watering the hope

New Year's Eve Anytime

Sheila and Mark make it a practice to celebrate New Year's Eve a little differently from the way other couples they know celebrate it. Sure, they get a babysitter for their two boys and head out for the evening, but they don't head to a friend's house for a party or to a loud nightclub. Instead, they find a quiet restaurant where they can have some extended quiet time together and do a "State of the Union" study of their marriage and family life during the past year. Is their marriage growing and getting stronger? Are the children doing well or having struggles? What changes do they want or need to make in the coming year? How do they sense God moving in their lives and guiding them as a couple?

After a nice meal and a long, undisturbed conversation, Sheila and Mark usually have a much better idea of the hopes and dreams that the other person has for the coming year. They are better able to work together toward the dreams that God has given them.

16. What benefits do you think Sheila and Mark experience as a result of intentionally planning for the future on their first date of the year?

17. List several questions that you would ask if you and your spouse had a dream date tonight.

That date sounds pretty good, doesn't it? Too bad it's not New Year's Eve! Of course, it doesn't matter whether or not it's New Year's Eve; what is important is to set some time aside to intentionally examine your life and dreams together with your spouse and to seek God together by asking Him what His plans and dreams for you are. It can be New Year's Eve anytime, even right now.

harvesting the fruit

Fostering good communication toward the future begins by remembering milestones of the past. Just as Psalm 136 served as a good reminder of God's blessings, you can write your own psalm that specifically applies to your marriage.

A Psalm to Remember

Follow the steps below to write your own psalm—a psalm of remembrance.

Step 1:   Make a list of the major milestones in your marriage.
Step 2:   Decide on a phrase that accurately describes how you feel about God's presence throughout the life of your marriage.
Step 3:   Write a psalm of remembrance, alternating between major milestones and the phrase that best describes your understanding of God's presence.

18. Talk with your spouse about what you learned from writing this psalm of remembrance.

God's Present

The following is a list of several gifts that God has given to you to help develop your marriage:

- Daily prayer together
- Weekly worship together
- A weekly date night
- A weekly fast for your marriage
- Individual Bible study
- Reading a book on marriage together
- A couples' Bible study
- Weekly marriage counseling
- A spiritual director
- Service to the poor, together as a couple

19. With your spouse, decide on two gifts that you will use every week for the next three months.

20. After deciding on the two gifts to "unwrap" over the next three months, make a plan to put them into action.

How will you use this gift?

When will you use it together?

Where will you use it regularly?

The Dream Date

It's time to start dreaming about how God wants to use your marriage to have a tremendous impact in the world. Share with your spouse your dreams, prayers, plans or ministry. Below are several questions that you can use to help guide the conversation with your spouse during your dream date. Remember, if you fail to plan, you plan to fail. This date is specifically for you to develop, dream and pray for God's direction in your marriage and the lives of your family. Although you may not cover all these questions, be sure to choose at least four and take time to adequately talk about how you both feel and think about what God might have in store for your marriage and your family.

Where do you feel God is challenging you and your spouse as a couple?

Where do you sense God challenging you individually?

If you could do any ministry with your spouse, what would it be?

What gifts has God given to you individually? What gifts has God given to you and your spouse as a couple?

What about your marriage would you like to change during the coming year?

What needs to change during the coming week?

If you have kids, how has your relationship with your spouse changed since adding children to your lives?

How has your relationship changed as the children have grown older?

What do you like about the changes that have happened since having children?

What do you not like about the changes that have happened since having children?

What do you appreciate about your spouse?

What would you like to change about yourself in order to better care for your spouse?

Hopefully, these questions will get your "dream juices" flowing. When you schedule a time to talk and dream, be sure to schedule plenty of time for conversation so that you don't feel rushed. Also, begin and end the date with prayer. In fact, you may want to light a candle at the beginning of the date as a symbol of God's light being with you as you talk.

Notes

1. Chinese proverb, quote at *About*. http://quotations.about.com/cs/inspirationquotes/a/responsibility (accessed May 10, 2005).

2. Johnson Oatman, Jr., "Count Your Blessings," quoted at *The Cyber Hymnal*. http://www.cyberhymnal. org/htm/c/o/countyou.htm (accessed August 2005).

3. Earl F. Palmer, *Revelation: The Communicator's Commentary* (Waco, TX: Word Books, 1982), p. 130.

4. Ibid.

leader's discussion guide

General Guidelines

1. If at all possible, the group should be led by a married couple. This does not mean that both spouses need to be leading the discussions—perhaps one spouse is better at facilitating discussions while the other is better at relationship building or organization—but the leader couple should share responsibilities wherever possible.

2. At the first meeting, be sure to lay down the ground rules for discussions, stressing that following these rules will help everyone feel comfortable during discussion times.

    a. No one should share anything of a personal or potentially embarrassing nature without first asking his or her spouse's permission.

    b. Whatever is discussed in the group meetings is to be held in strictest confidence among group members only.

    c. Allow everyone in the group to participate. However, as a leader, don't force anyone to answer a question if he or she is reluctant. Be sensitive to the different personalities and communication styles among your group members.

3. Fellowship time is very important in building small-group relationships. Providing beverages and/or light refreshments either before or after each session will encourage a time of informal fellowship.

4. Most people live very busy lives; respect the time of your group members by beginning and ending meetings on time.

The Focus on the Family Marriage Ministry Guide *has even more information on starting and leading a small group. You will find this an invaluable resource as you lead others through this Bible study.*

How to Use the Material

1. Each session has more than enough material to cover in a 45-minute teaching period. You will probably not have time to discuss every single question in each session, so prepare for each meeting by selecting questions you feel are most important to address for your group; discuss other questions as time permits. Be sure to save the last 10 minutes of your meeting time for each couple to interact individually and to pray together before adjourning.

   Optional Eight-Session Plan—You can easily divide each session into two parts if you'd like to cover all of the material presented in each session. Each section of the session has enough questions to divide in half, and the Bible study sections (Planting the Seed) are divided into two or three sections that can be taught in separate sessions. (You'll find more on how to do this in *The Focus on the Family Marriage Ministry Guide*.)

2. Each spouse should have his or her own copy of the book in order to personally answer the questions. The general plan of this study is that the couples complete the questions at home during the week and then bring their books to the meeting to share what they have learned during the week.

   However, the reality of leading small groups in this day and age is that some members will find it difficult to do the homework. If you find that to be the case with your group, consider adjusting the lessons and having members complete the study during your meeting time as you guide them through the lesson. If you use this method, be sure to encourage members to share their individual answers with their spouses during the week (perhaps on a date night).

Session One | Express Love Openly

Before the Meeting

1. If couples do not already know each other and/or you do not already know everyone's name, gather materials for making nametags.
2. Gather extra Bibles and pens or pencils for people to use during the study.
3. Make photocopies of the Prayer Request Form (see *The Focus on the Family Marriage Ministry Guide*, "Reproducible Forms" section) or provide 3x5-inch cards for recording requests. You may also want to have a notebook ready to record prayer requests and pray for each group member during the week.
4. Complete the study on your own during the week. Read through your own answers and mark the questions that you specifically want the group to discuss. As you prepare your answers, pray that God directs your discussion. Remember, there is more material than you may be able to cover with lively discussion, so be prepared to adjust accordingly.
5. Prepare slips of paper with the references for the Bible verses that will be read aloud during the session. Before you pass out these papers, you may want to ask in a friendly way whether some group members do not enjoy reading out loud.

Ice Breakers

1. Distribute Prayer Request Forms (or index cards) to members as they enter the room. Encourage them to complete their prayer requests before the session begins. If they do not have prayer requests or if they have never been to a Bible study before, just have them write their name on the paper so that others will be able to pray for them. Make members feel as comfortable as possible.
2. If this is the first time the group has met together, have each couple introduce themselves and tell the length of time they have been married, where they were married and maybe one interesting fact about themselves that others may not know. Be sure to remind couples that this is

not a time to embarrass their spouse. All stories should be shared with the permission of the spouse.

3. **Option 1:** Invite each couple to share about one of the best dates they have ever experienced, either while they were dating or after they were married.

   Option 2: Invite each couple to share the top two characteristics they appreciate about their spouse.

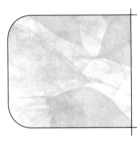

Note: Couples may be uncomfortable talking about their marriage during the first session. During this meeting, you may want to simply acknowledge that discomfort and gently encourage group members to share. As you share, you will model how to effectively communicate within the group.

4. Before beginning the study, be sure to pray for God's guidance and grace as you lead the group.

5. Read the introduction together as a group.

Discussion

1. **Tilling the Ground**—Ask a volunteer to read the commentary to get the group thinking about the different ways men and women communicate. Break into small groups (two couples in a group) and have them discuss questions 1 and 2. Encourage group members to think back to when they were dating. Bring the entire group back together and discuss questions 3 and 4. Question 4 will help the group understand the differences between how men and women have learned to express love.

2. **Planting the Seed**—Ask for a volunteer to read the introduction to this section. As a group, discuss question 5. Have each couple discuss question 6 individually. Bring the entire group together and discuss question 7. You may need to give an example of a list poem to help members understand how to answer question 8. Also, if you have colored markers and paper available, question 8 could become a creative project for the group. As you discuss questions 10 and 11, be sensitive that some members may still be learning to show expressions of love openly. Allow indi

vidual couples to discuss question 12 on their own.

3. **Watering the Hope**—After reading the case study together as a group, form small groups and discuss questions 13 through 15. When you sense the small groups have finished discussing these questions, have them come back together and report on one of their answers to the entire group.

4. **Harvesting the Fruit**—Couples will need individual time to discuss the four parts of questions 16. To keep this part moving and to give couples time to talk, lead the couples through each question. Ask the first question and let the couples talk for a period of time and then have them move on to the next question. This method will help group members who do not immediately feel as though they have something to share to consider how their parents expressed love. Bring the entire group together and discuss question 17. Again, have individual couples complete the rest of the session. Have each couple share what they intend to do this week on their date. You may also want to have each couple check in with another couple during the week to see how they are doing on following through on what they have learned at the study.

5. **Close in Prayer**—An important part of any small-group relationship is time spent in prayer for one another. This may be done in several ways:

   a. Have couples write specific prayer requests on the Prayer Request Forms (or index cards). These requests may be shared with the entire group or traded with another couple for the week. If requests are shared with the entire group, pray as a group before adjourning the meeting; if requests are traded, allow time for the prayer-partner couples to pray together.

   b. Gather the entire group together and lead couples in guided prayer, asking that God will continue to give them guidance as they share the exciting plan God has for their lives.

   c. Have individual couples pray together.

After the Meeting

1. **Evaluate**—Leaders should spend time evaluating the meeting's effectiveness (see *The Focus on the Family Marriage Ministry Guide*, "Reproducible Forms" section for an evaluation form).

2. **Encourage**—During the week, contact each couple (through phone calls, notes of encouragement, e-mail or instant messaging) and welcome them to the group. Make yourself available for answering any questions or concerns that they may have and to generally get to know them. This contact might best be done by the husband-leader contacting the men and the wife-leader contacting the women.

3. **Equip**—Complete the Bible study, even if you have previously gone through the study with your spouse.

4. **Pray**—Prayerfully prepare for the next meeting, praying for each couple and for your own preparation.

Session Two | Deal with Problems Honestly

Before the Meeting

1. Pray with your spouse and discuss how God has been working in your marriage during the past week.
2. Gather extra Bibles and pens or pencils for people to use during the study.
3. Make photocopies of the Prayer Request Form or provide 3x5-inch cards for recording requests. Bring your prayer journal or notebook and review prayer requests for the week.
4. As group members arrive, do an informal check-in or ask whether anyone wants to share how God answered prayers during the past week.
5. Complete the study on your own during the week. Read through your own answers and mark the questions that you specifically want the group to discuss. As you prepare, pray that God directs the group discussion and gives you insight into how to deal with problems in your own marriage.
6. Prepare slips of paper for the Scripture reference verses that you will want someone to read aloud during the session. Again, be sensitive to those who prefer not to read out loud.
7. You may also want to pick up a copy of *The Language of Love: How to Quickly Communicate Your Feelings and Needs* by Gary Smalley and John Trent to recommend to the group and read in preparation for this session.

Ice Breakers

1. Distribute Prayer Request Forms (or index cards) to members as they enter the meeting. Encourage them to complete their prayer requests before the session begins.
2. **Option 1:** Invite individual members to share about a time when they had a small problem that they did not deal with and it became a big problem. Let them know this instance could be anything from car problems to work problems to family problems.

   Option 2: Invite couples to share their experiences this week on their date or differences they noticed while expressing their love openly.

Option 3: Ask all members to recall when they were teenagers and identify the most typical problem a teenager faces and how a teenager usually deals with that problem.

3. Before beginning the study, be sure to pray for God's guidance and grace throughout the study.

Discussion

1. **Tilling the Ground**—Have a volunteer read the introduction. As a group, discuss questions 1 through 3. You may want to have newsprint available so that you can brainstorm as a group and write down members' responses. Invite group members to answer question 4 on their own. Have members share their responses if they are open to doing this.

2. **Planting the Seed**—As you discuss this section, be aware that some members in your group may not understand the depth of a relationship with God in Jesus Christ. Many couples rarely share their true feelings about God with one another. Encourage couples to think honestly about what it means to have God as a first love. Since Ephesians 4:25—5:2 will be used in sessions 2 and 3, you may want to read this passage aloud twice so that group members understand the importance of this text. Divide into small groups to discuss questions 7 through 10. Question 11 will allow group members to better understand a relationship with Jesus Christ. Be aware of God's movement to call members of the group closer to Him. Allow individual couples time to pray about question 12. You may also want to give each couple a candle to light as a representation of God's presence, which will help group members be attentive to the moving of God's Spirit as they pray.

3. **Watering the Hope**—If you have a copy of *The Language of Love: How to Quickly Communicate Your Feelings and Needs,* you may want to share more about word pictures before reading the case study. However, this section itself will help the group members learn a new form of communication. Ask couples to work in small groups to discuss the questions in this section and then have them come back to report to the entire group what they have learned from this experience.

4. **Harvesting the Fruit**—Allow time for each couple in the group to indi-

vidually discuss this section. You may want to reread Revelation 2 out loud to help each couple prepare. The couples will need some extended time to discuss these questions, so you may want to encourage them to schedule a time during the coming week to complete this section if they are unable to do so during this session. Have each couple choose another couple for them to check-in with during the coming week. A simple phone call or an e-mail is a great way for group members to encourage and pray for one another, and this will also help the members to stay focused during the week.

5. **Close in Prayer**—Have each couple pair up with another couple and share their prayer requests. Allow time for the foursomes to pray together and then close the meeting by praying for the couples.

After the Meeting

1. **Evaluate**—Leaders should spend time evaluating the meeting's effectiveness (see *The Focus on the Family Marriage Ministry Guide*, "Reproducible Forms" section for an evaluation form).
2. **Encourage**—Encourage prayer-partner couples to call each another during the week and inquire about their prayer concerns.
3. **Equip**—Complete the Bible Study.
4. **Pray**—Prayerfully prepare for the next meeting, praying for each couple and for your own preparation.

Session Three | Express Emotions Appropriately

Before the Meeting

1. Pray with your spouse and discuss how God has been working in your marriage during the past week. Discuss any changes you have seen in your ability to talk about your problems honestly. Remember, God will use this study to enhance and enrich your marriage.
2. Check in with group members during the week either through an e-mail or a phone call.
3. Gather extra Bibles and pens or pencils for people to use during the study.
4. Make photocopies of the Prayer Request Form (see *The Focus on the Family Marriage Ministry Guide*, "Reproducible Forms" section) or provide 3x5-inch index cards for recording requests. Bring your prayer journal or notebook and review prayer requests for the week. As group members arrive, do an informal check-in or you can ask whether anyone wants to share how God answered prayers during the past week.
5. Complete the study on your own during the week. Read through your own answers and mark the questions that you specifically want the group to discuss. With your spouse, pray for the members of the group for whom God may specifically be calling you to care for. As you prepare, pray that God will give you direction during the discussion section.
6. Prepare slips of paper with the references for the Bible verses that you want to have read aloud during the session. Again, be sensitive to those who prefer not to read out loud.

Ice Breakers

1. Distribute Prayer Request Forms (or index cards) to members as they enter the meeting. Encourage group members to complete their prayer requests before the session begins.
2. **Option 1:** Invite couples to share how they experienced talking honestly about the problems affecting their marriage. It will be important to note that if there are deep issues facing some marriages of the couples in your

group, this week's session may have been very difficult for those couples. Encourage group members to pray and be aware that group prayer is a process of growing closer.

Option 2: Invite individual group members to share about a time when they felt intense joy, anger or sadness about a situation in their childhood.

Option 3: Invite individual group members to complete one of the following sentences: "I feel the most joy when I . . ."; "I feel the deepest sadness when . . ."

3. Before beginning the study, pray for God's guidance and grace throughout the study.

Discussion

1. **Tilling the Ground**—Have a volunteer read the opening paragraphs. Take a moment to allow people to think about the two quotations and what they mean. Discuss question 1 as a group. Questions 2 and 3 should be discussed in small groups. If you have newsprint available, write the list from question 4 on the newsprint so that the entire group can quietly consider it.

2. **Planting the Seed**—Divide couples into small groups and have them discuss question 5. When they've discussed all the psalms, have one person from each couple talk briefly about which passage had an impact on them. As a group, read Psalm 55 out loud slowly. After reading it, allow group members to read it a second time quietly and then have them answer question 6. Discuss questions 7 and 8 together as a group. It will be important to highlight the difference between David's emotional response to an enemy and Jesus' response. Discuss questions 11 through 15 as a group and then let individual couples discuss question 16 together.

3. **Watering the Hope**—Have each couple read the case study and discuss questions 17 and 18 individually. Gather the entire group together to discuss question 19. Be sure to discuss the differences among passive, assertive and aggressive responses.

4. **Harvesting the Fruit**—Read through the commentary together as a group. It will be very important that the group members feel the

presence of Christ as they work through this section. Prayer will be critical. Pray individually for each couple as they work through this section. Have each couple individually discuss question 21, and encourage them to be honest and gracious. Gather the entire group together and explain questions 22 and 23. Reread Ephesians 4:25—5:2 to lay the groundwork; then divide the couples into small groups to discuss questions 22 and 23.

5. **Close in Prayer**—Have each couple pair up with another couple to share their prayer requests. Allow time for the foursomes to pray together and then close the meeting by praying for the couples.

After the Meeting

1. **Evaluate**—Leaders should spend time evaluating the meeting's effectiveness (see *The Focus on the Family Marriage Ministry Guide*, "Reproducible Forms" section for an evaluation form).
2. **Encourage**—Encourage prayer-partner couples to call one another during the week and inquire about their prayer concerns.
3. **Equip**—Complete the Bible study.
4. **Pray**—Prayerfully prepare for the next meeting, praying for each couple and for your own preparation.

Session Four | Remember the Past and Dream for the Future

Before the Meeting

1. During the week, pray with your spouse and discuss how God has been working in your marriage this week. Reflect on how God has been working on relationships in your individual lives and in your life as a couple.

2. Gather extra Bibles and pens or pencils for people to use during the study.

3. Check in with the group members during the week via phone or e-mail. You may want to ask group members whether they would be interested in another study.

4. Make photocopies of the Prayer Request Form (see *The Focus on the Family Marriage Ministry Guide*, "Reproducible Forms" section) or provide 3x5-inch index cards for recording requests. As group members enter, be sure to check in to see how God has been working through prayer in their lives.

5. Complete the study on your own during the week. Read through your own answers and mark the questions that you specifically want the group to discuss. As you prepare your answers, pray that God will direct your discussion. You may want to have a dream date with your spouse sometime during the week as a way to prepare for this study.

6. If your group has access to a guitar or a piano, you may want to have the group sing the hymn "Count Your Blessings" to introduce the "Tilling the Ground" section.

7. Prepare slips of paper with the references for the Bible verses that you will want someone to read aloud during the session. Be sensitive to those who prefer not to read out loud.

Ice Breakers

1. **Option 1:** Ask the group to answer one of the following questions:
   - What's the best memory you have from when you were dating?
   - What experience have you had recently that you think will become an outstanding memory?

Option 2: Ask the group members to share how the study has had an impact on their ability to communicate in their marriage.

Option 3: Read the Chinese proverb that appears at the beginning of the session, and have each member tell how that statement could be true in his or her own life.

2.   Before beginning the study, be sure to pray for God's guidance and grace through the study.

3.   Read the opening paragraphs out loud as a group.

Discussion

1.   **Tilling the Ground**—Give each couple time to answer questions 1 and 2 together, and then invite them to talk to the group about one of their experiences of God's blessings. Have an experience prepared for question 3 and ask whether others would like to share a defining moment. A twist to question 3 would be to have the spouse of the person talking about a defining moment to share how he or she experienced God's working. Have fun with question 4, but be sensitive to the couples in the group who are engaged.

2.   **Planting the Seed**—Have one member read the leading phrases in Psalm 136 and have the other group members respond with "His love endures forever." Allow time for group members to respond to question 6, and then invite volunteers to share their responses.

   In preparation for reading Deuteronomy 6:1-12, it may be helpful to summarize God's work in the lives of the Israelites after God led them out of bondage. Divide the group into small groups, and then have each small group discuss question 9. Have each group share what it found in the text. Gather the entire group together and discuss question 10. Then have each couple discuss question 11 individually. Question 13 can be used as a way to elicit prayer requests from each couple; however, you may want them to answer this question in small groups. Encourage each couple to make a commitment to pray for each other after this study has ended. If possible, light a candle as a sign of God's presence, creating a moment of silence so that couples can listen for God's Spirit; then discuss question 15.

3.   **Watering the Hope**—Read the case study aloud. If you and your spouse

had a dream date before this meeting, share what you learned from your experience. Discuss question 16 as a group, and then give couples time to answer question 17 individually. If you have newsprint, write down all the questions from each couple so that group members can learn from one another.

4. **Harvesting the Fruit**—After the couples have written their psalms of remembrance, invite them to share their psalm with the whole group. Be sensitive to those who may not want to share. Couples may want to read their psalms together, similar to the way you read Psalm 136 as a group earlier in the study. The final two sections, "God's Present" and "The Dream Date," should be discussed by each couple individually. Encourage couples to share with the entire group what they plan to do, and then invite them to share with another couple sometime after the study how they are following God daily and what happened during their dream date. Remember to encourage each couple to continue to apply principles they have learned.

5. **Close in Prayer**—Use this time as a way of bringing closure to the group. Pray together with the entire group and have couples pray specifically for the other couples to grow deeper in their relationship with Christ. After praying, talk about what each couple will do to continue to grow in their relationship with one another.

After the Meeting

1. **Evaluate**—Distribute the Study Evaluation Form (see *The Focus on the Family Marriage Ministry Guide*, "Reproducible Forms" section) for group members to take home with them. Share the importance of feedback and ask members to take time this week to write their review of the group meetings and them return them to you.

2. **Encourage**—Call each couple during the week and invite them to join you for the next study in the Focus on the Family Marriage Series.

3. **Equip**—Begin preparing and brainstorming activities for the next Bible study.

4. **Pray**—Give thanks to the Lord for the work he has done in the lives of the couples in the study. Continue to pray for these couples as they apply the lessons learned in the last few weeks.

STRENGTHEN MARRIAGES.
STRENGTHEN YOUR CHURCH.
Here's Everything You Need for a Dynamic Marriage Ministry!

Group Starter Kit includes

- Nine Bible Studies: *The Masterpiece Marriage, The Passionate Marriage, The Fighting Marriage, The Model Marriage, The Surprising Marriage, The Giving Marriage, The Covenant Marriage, The Abundant Marriage* and *The Blended Marriage*
- *The Focus on the Family Marriage Ministry Guide*
- *An Introduction to the Focus on the Family Marriage Series* video

Focus on the Family®
Marriage Series
Group Starter Kit
Kit Box
Bible Study/Marriage
ISBN 08307.32365

The overall health of your church is directly linked to the health of its marriages. And in light of today's volatile pressures and changing lifestyles, your commitment to nurture and strengthen marriages needs tangible, practical help. Now **Focus on the Family—the acknowledged leader in Christian marriage and family resources**—gives churches a comprehensive group study series dedicated to enriching marriages. Strengthen marriages and strengthen your church with **The Focus on the Family Marriage Series.**

The Focus on the Family Marriage Series
is available at bookstores everywhere.

Gospel Light

Don't Miss These Other Great Marriage Resources from the Focus on the Family Marriage Series

The Masterpiece Marriage
ISBN 08307.31202

The Covenant Marriage
ISBN 08307.31199

The Passionate Marriage
ISBN 08307.31520

The Fighting Marriage
ISBN 08307.31490

The Model Marriage
ISBN 08307.31504

The Surprising Marriage
ISBN 08307.31539

The Giving Marriage
ISBN 08307.31512

The Blended Marriage
ISBN 08307.33213

The Abundant Marriage
ISBN 08307.33205

New from Focus on the Family®

The Women's Ministry That Has It All!

Kit includes
- *The Focus on the Family Women's Ministry Guide*
- *Crafts and Activities for Women's Ministry*
- *Women of Worth* Bible Study
- *Healing the Heart* Bible Study
- *Balanced Living* Bible Study
- *The Blessings of Friendships* Bible Study

Focus on the Family Women's Series Kit
Group Starter Kit • Bible Study
ISBN 08307.33574

Research shows that women are the backbone of Christian congregations in America,*
but many are overwhelmed and in need of a break to reconnect with the Lord.
Focus on the Family has **combined the best features of women's ministries—**
Bible studies, prayer, fellowship, Scripture memory and activities—and created
new resources for women of all ages so that they can *relax* and *reflect* on God.

By learning to define themselves based on God's Word, women will decrease
their feelings of being inadequate and overwhelmed, and increase their sense of
self-worth while joining in fellowship with God and other Christian women.
Help women come together with **the new ministry that has it all!**

The Focus on the Family Women's Series
is available at bookstores everywhere.

Gospel Light

*From Barna Research, *Women Are the Backbone of the Christian Congregations in America*, March 6, 2000.